JOHN & EDWARD RULE, OK!

THE RISE AND RISE OF

THE NATION'S FAVOURITE TWINS.

WRITTEN BY CHAS NEWKEY-BURDEN

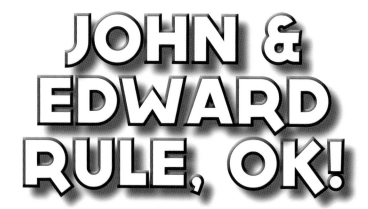

JOHN & EDWARD RULE, OK!

A Pillar Box Red Publication

© 2011. Published by Pillar Box Red Publishing Ltd.

ISBN 978-1-907823-26-8

Images © bigpictures.co.uk

CONTENTS

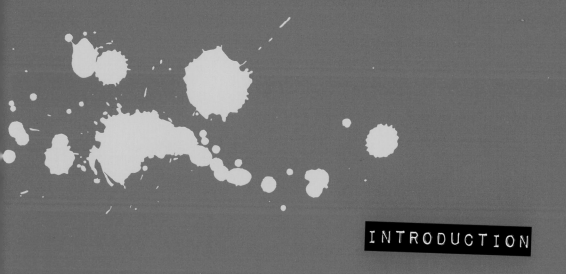

How did John and Edward Grimes go from being **The X Factor** outsiders to having chart success and enduring popularity? This revealing and entertaining book shows how these energetic, fun-loving Irish lads made their dreams of fame come true.

Taking the story from their premature birth and schooling right up to their smash-hit second album and hilarious **Celebrity Big Brother** antics, this book reveals the real John and Edward Grimes for the first time.

This inspiring, gripping story of how they overcame countless obstacles will delight all Jedward fans. So turn the page, and let the caper-filled fun begin.

The Early Birds

John and Edward Grimes are always at their best when the odds are against them. Whatever life has thrown at them they have proved that nothing can keep them down. They are true survivors, as they showed from the very start of their lives. It was in the springtime of 1991 that their parents, John and Susanna, found out Susanna was expecting twins. Doctors told the excited couple that the twin boys were due around Christmas time 1991. The boys had other ideas, though.

They were born early, on 16th October, in Dublin's Rotunda Hospital. Their premature arrival came just 31 weeks into Susanna's pregnancy. Babies are usually born in the 40th week. John arrived first, and weighed only 4lbs. Edward came along 10 minutes later, weighing 5lbs. Doctors rushed the premature babies straight to an incubator so the hospital staff could care for and monitor them. The incubator was to be their home for some weeks. These were tense times for the Grimes family: premature babies do not always survive long after their birth. In fact, doctors gave John and Edward only a 50/50 chance of surviving.

Their parents crossed their fingers, and thankfully the babies who would become Ireland's most famous twins did indeed survive. As their Dad John later told The Mirror: 'They were so small

and fragile but thankfully they pulled through.' The baby John was the first to be declared ready to go home. His brother Edward followed the next week. They joined their older brother Kevin, who had himself been born prematurely. Indeed, you could say the Grimes family is one of many miracles.

John and Edward were born under the star sign of Libra. According to astrologers, this should make them charming people, who love artistic and creative pursuits including music. Most of their fans would agree they have kept true to all of that. Another characteristic associated with Librans is that they are said to enjoy being centre of the attention. There can be little doubt that applies to John and Edward.

They grew up in a small Irish town called Rathangan, in County Kildare. The neighbourhood sits quietly on the banks of the Slate River. There is also a Grand Canal, meaning the area has lots of opportunities for anglers. John and Edward were more interested in mischief-making. When they look back, they compare their childhood selves to the cheeky, impish Beano character Dennis the Menace. It's an accurate comparison; they were often up to no good.

Even as they showed their creative side they made mischief. Both were keen on drawing as kids but sometimes their efforts with crayons and markers would go beyond the pages of their colouring-in books and onto the walls of the house. Later, they drew on their desks in the classroom when their interest in a lesson dropped off. They enjoyed some parts of school, though. Art was John's favourite lesson at school, both of them enjoyed maths sometimes too.

Both had vivid imaginations and were easily scared. They worried that their cuddly toys would come to life in the night and turn into monsters. Even the clothes in their bedroom closet would haunt them at night because the twins thought they looked like people hanging from the rail. It was their Mum and Dad's turn to be scared when a game of hide-and-seek went wrong. John and Edward - then just three years of age - hid under the family car. As they searched frantically, their parents worried that their beloved twin boys had been abducted. When they got their first bicycles, their unannounced cycling expeditions also worried Susanna who wondered where they had gone.

There were mishaps in John and Edward's childhood but they were usually fairly minor. While on holiday in Wexford, John slipped over in the bed-and-breakfast they were staying in and landed hard against a window. During another holiday, it was their big brother's turn for drama. The three boys were playing on a big open field when Kevin suddenly disappeared. One moment he had been there, the next he was nowhere to be seen. It turned out he had fallen down a well. Their cousin Matt had to come and save him.

At Christmas time they would often stay with their grandparents. When the weather turned freezing, John and Edward loved to create a mini ice-rink by pouring buckets of water onto the pavement outside the door. They were so excited as they saw the water quickly turn to ice. Neighbours and other visitors were less thrilled when they slipped on the ice. When their Dad slipped one day he let his feelings be known. Back at the family home voices were raised when John broke a window during a football kick-around in the garden. The kids loved the garden and remember to this day the beautiful, multi-coloured rose bushes in the front garden that captured their attention from an early age.

Some of their first musical experiences came in the car as they were driven to school each morning. It would often be country music that was played. John and Edward quickly learned the lyrics and would sing along in the back seats. These early morning drives were the first Jedward concerts. They also loved pop music, with Robbie Williams, NSYNC, Britney Spears and the Backstreet Boys among their favourite acts.

When they were six years of age they were given their very first musical instruments: John got a guitar and Edward a violin. They joined the choir at school and quickly loved the experience of singing to an audience. At home they would perform imaginary concerts in their bedrooms, with their cuddly toys lined-up as an 'audience'. They loved real animals too and were excited when the family took in a dog called Trixie, who had been found abandoned in Dublin. They later added pet cats, a budgie and a pony called Dusty to their collection. Like Trixie, Dusty had been abandoned by a previous owner too. The twin boys loved giving all their pets the love and attention they deserved.

Still, another moment of mischief was never far away. One day Edward hopped onto his grandfather's lawnmower car and tried to take it for an impromptu spin. He managed to get it started but like a scene straight out of a comedy he drove straight into the neighbour's hedge. On another day, John lifted Edward into a wheelbarrow and walked off, leaving him stuck there for some time. Edward said he was 'really freaked out'.

However, among the pranks and cheekiness, the twins were showing that they did not lack another personality trait. Having been born prematurely and spent weeks together in an incubator, they had developed an unshakeable bond and love for each other. Even by the standards of twins, they were close. Photographs of their childhood which the twins have posted on their Twitter page show them bathing together as toddlers looking both cute and close.

Far from wanting independence or space, they absolutely loved being close to one another. When the family moved house their parents told them they could have their own rooms in the new place. The parents thought the boys might be delighted by this turn of events, but John and Edward quickly found they missed one another. Within days, Edward had moved into John's room where they slept in bunk beds.

Twins are often very close, but the bond between John and Edward was particularly strong from the start. At school they preferred each other's company to that of any classmates. It was always a case of John and Edward against the world. Their early arrival into the world and the way they survived their premature birth suggested they were two plucky boys who were in a hurry to live life to the full.

However, their childhood was not without its trials and tribulations. They boys always stood out of the crowd thanks to their energetic and fun-loving natures. As they moved through school they found that not everyone appreciated this.

CHAPTER TWO
Time to Face the Music

At the age of eight, John and Edward were sent to the King's Hospital boarding school. It is one of the best schools in Ireland but sadly the twins were targeted by bullies there. 'Everyone experiences tough times in their lives and we're no different,' John told The Mirror referring to what happened to them there. 'I think a lot of people will be able to relate to what we went through.'

The bullying was both verbal and physical. The fact they were twins and also full of life made them stand out from the start. They were also very confident with talking to girls, something that also made some fellow male pupils jealous of them. Although they faced some unpleasant treatment, their experiences again only made them closer to one another. Four years after enrolling at King's Hospital they were moved to a new school and have been much happier since.

Meanwhile, as they entered their teenage years the boyhood rites of passage continued. Although neither twin has ever had a proper girlfriend, John remembers his first kiss with a girl. 'I was walking with her, suddenly she stopped and wrapped her arms around me,' John told The Sun. 'I felt her heart flutter, we stared at each other in shock, then we kissed.' Soon, Edward remembered, girls were fighting with each other for the attention of the boys.

They took part in lots of extra activities at school from running and canoeing to music and drama. That famous 'Jedward energy' meant they were always ready for the next bit of fun. They won the hearts of more girls when they took part in a school talent show in 2006. They sang *I Want It That Way* by their beloved Backstreet Boys and drew cheers and screams of admiration from the audience. When they posted a video of the performance on YouTube it quickly attracted very positive comments from people who watched the video. They had enjoyed their time in the limelight and hoped they could return under its glare in the future.

In 2008, they took on a massive challenge for charity. They decided to climb the four biggest mountains in Ireland, England, Wales and Scotland to raise money for charity. They had to train very hard for such a physical and mental challenge. During the training and the climbs themselves the boys grew closer as they went through the highs and lows together. They were proving real young action heroes: having joined a running club they were competing in and sometimes winning regional running events.

There was even talk of them training for the Olympic Games. However, a competition of a different sort was beckoning the twins. In 2008, like millions of other people John and Edward were gripped by the ITV talent show *The X Factor*. They watched from home as London soul singer Alexandra Burke swept to victory in one of the most exciting ever series of the contest. They had also enjoyed following the journeys of other contestants, including the boy band JLS and the baby-faced young singer from Northern Ireland, Eoghan Quigg.

It all looked so fun and exciting. So, when their Grandad suggested they audition themselves the following year, the twins decided that was a good idea. They had done well in school singing contests and still dreamt of becoming famous as a duo. *The X Factor,* which prides itself on giving a chance to ambitious hopefuls who might otherwise be ignored by the music industry, seemed to be a great way to have a crack at that. It felt like destiny was calling them. So they filled in the form and counted down the days to their first audition.

That audition was to be in front of the show's producers, in London. The boys made enough of an impression to be invited back to audition in front of Simon Cowell and the other judges in Glasgow. In between the two auditions they continued to prepare for their big chance in front of the famous *X Factor* panel. The 2009 series was the first one in which auditions took place in front of an arena audience, so they would have thousands of audience members watching them as well as the dreaded judges.

Far from showing any nerves on the big day, the twins instead appeared on stage oozing confidence. They asked the thousands of audience members if they were ready to party. It was certainly a bold entrance! They had the attention of the judges right away. 'Who have we got here?' asked Louis Walsh.

Edward replied: 'We're twins, I'm Edward...'

Then John added: 'I'm John, we're 17 and we're from Dublin.'

Cheryl, noting that they were Irish like Walsh, jokingly said: 'It's a yes from Louis.'

Then, the notorious Simon Cowell spoke, and his words were suitably withering: 'Guys, why are you talking in American accents?' John replied: 'It's the way it sounds over a microphone.'

Cheryl then moved the conversation on. 'Where do you see yourselves in 15 years time?' she asked. John, quick as a flash, replied: 'Well I see myself being older.' They had not even sung yet

and the twins had already made a huge impact with their cheeky responses to the judges' remarks. When it came to sing, they parted from each other's sides to sing their song, **As Long As You Love Me**, by the Backstreet Boys.

As the verse moved into the chorus, they encouraged the audience to sing along with them. They were behaving like established stars, as if their audition was actually a live show that they were headlining. Whatever else you could say about them, you could not doubt their confidence. Nobody was going to forget this audition in a hurry. However, head judge Simon Cowell cut them off before they had even finished the chorus. The boys held their breaths as Cowell delivered his verdict: 'Not very good, and incredibly annoying.' Cheryl said that there was something 'intriguing' about the twins, but added that she did not know if it was in a good way or not. It wasn't going well for the boys.

Louis then spoke. The boys were hoping for a better comment from their fellow Irishman. 'You really do look like pop stars, you know?' he told them, much to Simon's disgust. 'I think you've got something,' added Walsh. Dannii then described them as 'absolutely the cockiest couple of singers I've ever come across yet'. Louis differed, saying they were 'cheeky rather than cocky'. Dannii then added: 'I like you guys'.

Which way was this going? When it came time to vote on whether to put them through, Simon said 'no', but Cheryl and Dannii both said 'yes'. So it came down to Louis to cast the deciding vote. He told them he was putting them through to the next round. So through they went to the 'boot camp' phase, with 100 other acts. First, they sang Michael Jackson's **You Are Not Alone**. Looking smart in grown-up shirts and ties, they sang the sweet song gently and seriously. This was a different John and Edward to the ones that had first appeared. Louis said later this was the first time that the judges realised the boys could sing well. When the twins learned they had made it through to the next stage of boot camp, they said they were 'stunned'.

They were put into a group with three female singers. They sang **Apologise**, by Timbaland. Naturally, John and Edward refused to sink into the background for this group performance and instead made sure they were centre of attention by clowning around. John had even arrived on-stage doing a cartwheel. After the group song, Sian accused them of singing over her. Cowell had noticed that and took the boys to task for it. However, Louis defended them again, saying they had 'potential' and adding 'I think kids are going to like you guys'. Simon disagreed, calling them 'nasty brats'. However, the boys were again voted through against Simon's wishes. They leapt off the stage in

celebration - they'd done it! The next round was the judge's houses phase. This meant that they only had one more hurdle to clear in order to qualify for the live shows which were watched and voted on by millions of television viewers every Saturday night. Even before their ultimate fate was decided, the boys had already become one of the main talking points of the series. Some viewers loved them, some hated them - but everybody had noticed them.

Initially, acts are not told which of the judge's houses they would be visiting. So when they flew to Italy and then were driven to a villa in Lake Como, they did not know which judge would be deciding their fate. They were delighted when they learned it was Louis Walsh. He had been their biggest champion in the show to date so they had high hopes he would judge them favourably. Not only that, he had also managed successful Irish boy bands such as Boyzone and Westlife. What better man to have on their side?

Alongside Walsh as his assistant for the judging was Boyzone frontman Ronan Keating. In front of two of Ireland's most successful pop figures, the boys sang *I Want It That Way*. John's vocals went slightly wrong at one point in the chorus, but they had done enough to go through to the live shows. When they were told they had reached the next stage the boys jumped up and down with joy and hugged one another. Not for the first time in their lives they had defied the odds and won.

They were through to the live shows.

Live and Loud

Even before the live shows kicked-off, John and Edward were already one of the most-discussed **X Factor** acts in history. Some people loved them, some people disliked them but everybody seemed to have an opinion of them. They received fan-mail by the sack load before the first live show and the media could not stop discussing these two striking boys from Ireland. All of this gave them great encouragement as they rehearsed for up to 10 hours a day.

In the first live show they sang **Rock DJ** by Robbie Williams. From their attention-grabbing entrance from the ceiling to the last note, it was classic Jedward. All the judges praised the boys for their strength in the face of some of the nasty comments they had faced in recent weeks. Cheryl Cole told them they could not sing and Cowell told them their performance was 'a musical nightmare'. However, when the public vote was announced the next night they sailed through to the next week.

Indeed, it was not until week five that the boys were first left in the dreaded bottom two. Their spectacular performance of **Ghostbusters** had even drawn a compliment from Cowell and when the voting was taken to deadlock, they were saved. The following week they sang a mash-up of the

Queen song **Under Pressure** and the Vanilla Ice track **Ice Ice Baby.** Again, they avoided the bottom two. However, in week seven their **X Factor** journey came to an end. They were in the bottom two with popular male solo contestant Olly Murs. This time, the judges chose to eliminate the twins.

After the rollercoaster ride of *The X Factor*, John and Edward might have expected to have a rest. However, as they quickly found out - there would be no rest for the Jedward. As they left the show, their mentor Louis Walsh told them that this was not the end but the beginning for them. He was true to his word, and they signed a management deal with him. This meant that they had their biggest champion taking care of their career ahead.

'I've always been convinced that they have a great career ahead of them,' Louis told the BBC as he announced the deal. His prediction that they had bright things to come was proved right when they quickly signed a one-track record deal with Sony Music and then were approached by ITV2 who wanted to make a documentary about their day-to-day lives as young stars. They were getting the sort of attention that an *X Factor* winner would expect to receive.

Imagine their excitement as they skipped into the studio to record their debut single. They chose to make it the 'mash-up' of two songs they had sung on *The X Factor*: the Queen track *Under Pressure* and Vanilla Ice's song *Ice Ice Baby*. They almost burst with delight when Vanilla Ice agreed to contribute his own vocals to the single. He had seen them on the YouTube website and enjoyed their sense of fun. Having this hip-hop legend joining them on the single was just the "icing" on the cake for the boys.

When the single was released at the end of January, it immediately sold well to their growing army of admirers. It went straight to number one in Ireland and reached number two in the UK. The outsiders of *The X Factor*, who had been booed and mocked by some viewers, were now standing tall. Their first public performance of the song came at the National Television Awards at the O2 in London. Their performance, with Vanilla Ice joining them on-stage, was the highlight of the night. Backstage afterwards Vanilla Ice showered the twins with praise, saying: 'They are at the cutting edge.'

It had been a great start for the twins. Their first single had sold brilliantly and they appeared on a handful of top television shows including *Friday Night With Jonathan Ross* and the huge Irish show *The Late Late Toy Show*. Ross loved them and he was far from the only celebrity to have an opinion on the new twins on the block. Everyone from clean-cut teen heartthrob Justin Bieber to hell-raising The Pogues front-man Shane MacGowan expressed their respect for the lads. Even the leader of the Conservative Party David Cameron admitted he always looked forward to their appearances. The public was no less fascinated: everywhere John and Edward went they were instantly recognised and mobbed by screaming fans.

Although the boys were exhausted after the relentless pressure of the live **X Factor** shows, they were not to get any chance to rest in the years ahead. Such was the public and media demand for Jedward that they soon had a schedule that would, in the words of their manager, 'make your eyes water' it was so packed and demanding. First-up came the live **X Factor** tour, in which the leading contestants toured Britain's biggest venues to perform in-person for the show's fans. Despite not having reached the top three of the show, the boys stole the show on many nights of the 50-date tour.

At one of the shows, at London's O2 Arena, among the audience were some leading executives from Universal Records. They decided to sign Jedward to a full deal to record their debut album. It was called **Planet Jedward** and was released in the summer of 2010. The track-list consisted entirely of cover versions of well-known pop and rock songs: everything from **All The Small Things** by Blink 182 to **Fight For Your Right** by the Beastie Boys. Each track was given the full, fun Jedward treatment. It went to number one in Ireland where it reached presitigious 'double platinum' status, the top 20 in the UK and even charted in other European countries.

By this time, Jedward had followed-up *The X Factor* tour with their first solo tour. Across 27 nights of screaming, fun and frolics, they rocked venues across Ireland. So many fans had tried to buy tickets that the boys had to add a list of additional dates just to cope with the demand. The levels of excitement in the audience was so frenzied that one newspaper compared it to that which greeted The Beatles at their height. 'Jedwardmania is right up there with Beatlemania,' said the *Irish Independent*. More than ever in their eventful, rollercoaster life, everything seemed to be going their way. However, another challenge was just round the corner. Would Jedward be able to overcome it this time?

In August, a performance at the *T4 On The Beach* show ended in disaster when Edward slipped on-stage and seriously injured his leg. It was during their medley performance, that Edward fatefully slipped. He was in so much pain. At first, John did not realise what had happened to his beloved twin. Then he realised, and as the music track continued, he said: 'You've hurt your leg. Are you all right man?' Edward replied: 'I'm cool.' Courageously and professionally, Edward continued with the performance as planned.

This was the Jedward spirit at its most indomitable and admirable. After their on-stage slot ended poor Edward was helped off the stage as an ambulance was called. He was then rushed to the Weston General Hospital in the resort to have his injured leg examined. It was quickly discovered that he would need surgery to repair his knee. As he recovered after surgery John was very supportive of his younger twin. Edward received messages of support from thousands of fans and also from fellow music artists who were impressed with how he handled the on-stage injury.

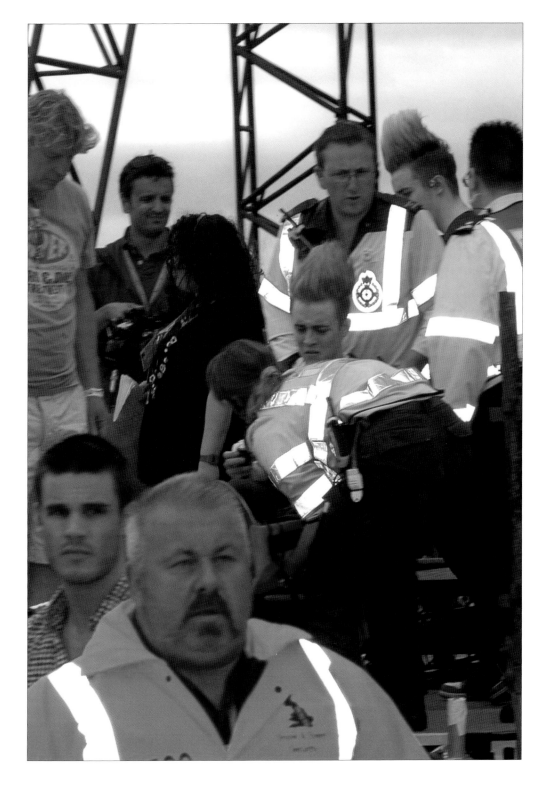

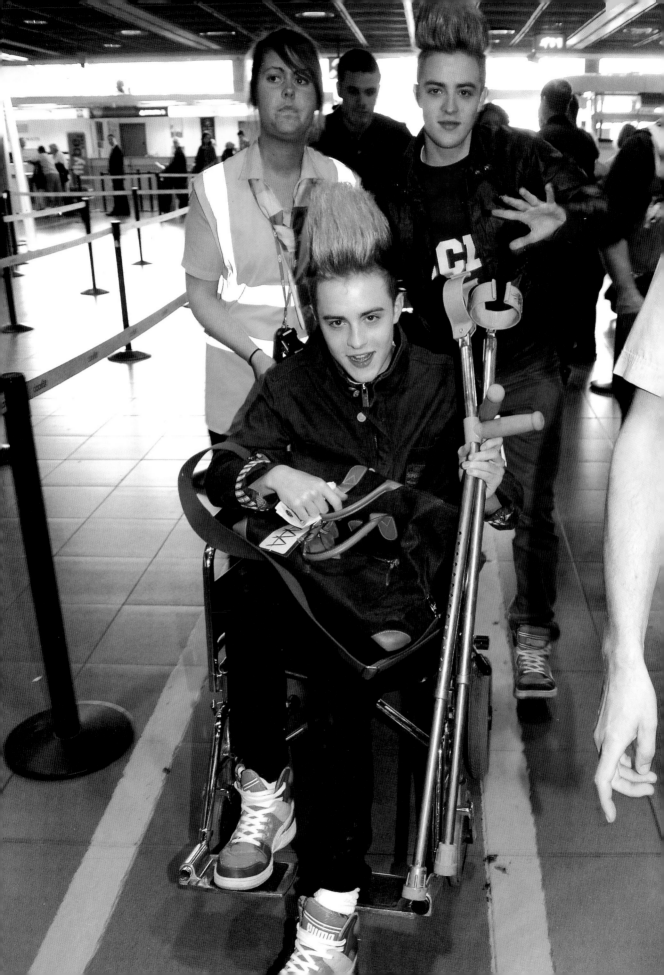

Meanwhile, the show went on. Throughout 2010, Jedward were invited to endorse all manner of products. Companies across the UK and Ireland were keen to bring a bit of the twins' fun and fame to their own products. The carpet cleaning brand Shake n' Vac was one such lucrative deal they struck. Their energetic promotion of the product made it relevant again in the 21st century, as well as putting a smile on the faces of those who used it while doing the household tasks. The twins also launched merchandise of their own, including Jedward Easter eggs. All of this was earning them big bucks. Louis Walsh had promised to make them millionaires and already they were well on their way to seeing that magical figure on their bank statements.

They also broke their first world record when they hid inside a large gift-wrapped box as part of the final layer of the world's largest Pass-the-Parcel. They burst out, dressed as the **Toy Story** hero Buzz Lightyear. They had been inside the parcel for 40 minutes, so were even more excitable than usual as they finally broke free. Afterwards, the Guinness World Record judge handed her business card to the boys and asked them to get in touch if they had any ideas in the future for other records they could break or set. Among the ideas they have toyed with are records for the world's tallest hair, or sticking the most chewing gum on one another.

By the end of 2010, their first full year in the public eye, their list of achievements seemed to have no end. They had been photographed in **Vogue** and **Grazia** magazines, appeared in the pantomime show **Cinderella**, they had performed to 80,000 people in Dublin as support act to the mighty Westlife, appeared on countless top TV entertainment shows and been featured in their own mini-series, **Jedward Let Loose**. The three-part show began in August. It followed their lives as they released and promoted their debut album.

However, they had also tasted tragedy during the year, when their beloved grandfather Kevin had died. They had loved him so much and were devastated when he passed away. They proudly carried his coffin at the funeral in Lucan, Ireland. As they grieved alongside their relatives, John and Edward paid tribute to the enormous influence their grandfather had on their development as people. They also became ever more determined to honour his memory by living their lives to the full.

Nothing could detract from their incredible achievements during the year. It had been a truly amazing 12 months, beyond even their excitable and ambitious dreams. More amazing still was that in 2011 they would surpass all of those achievements, as the Jedward juggernaut shifted into an even higher gear.

Vanilla Ice

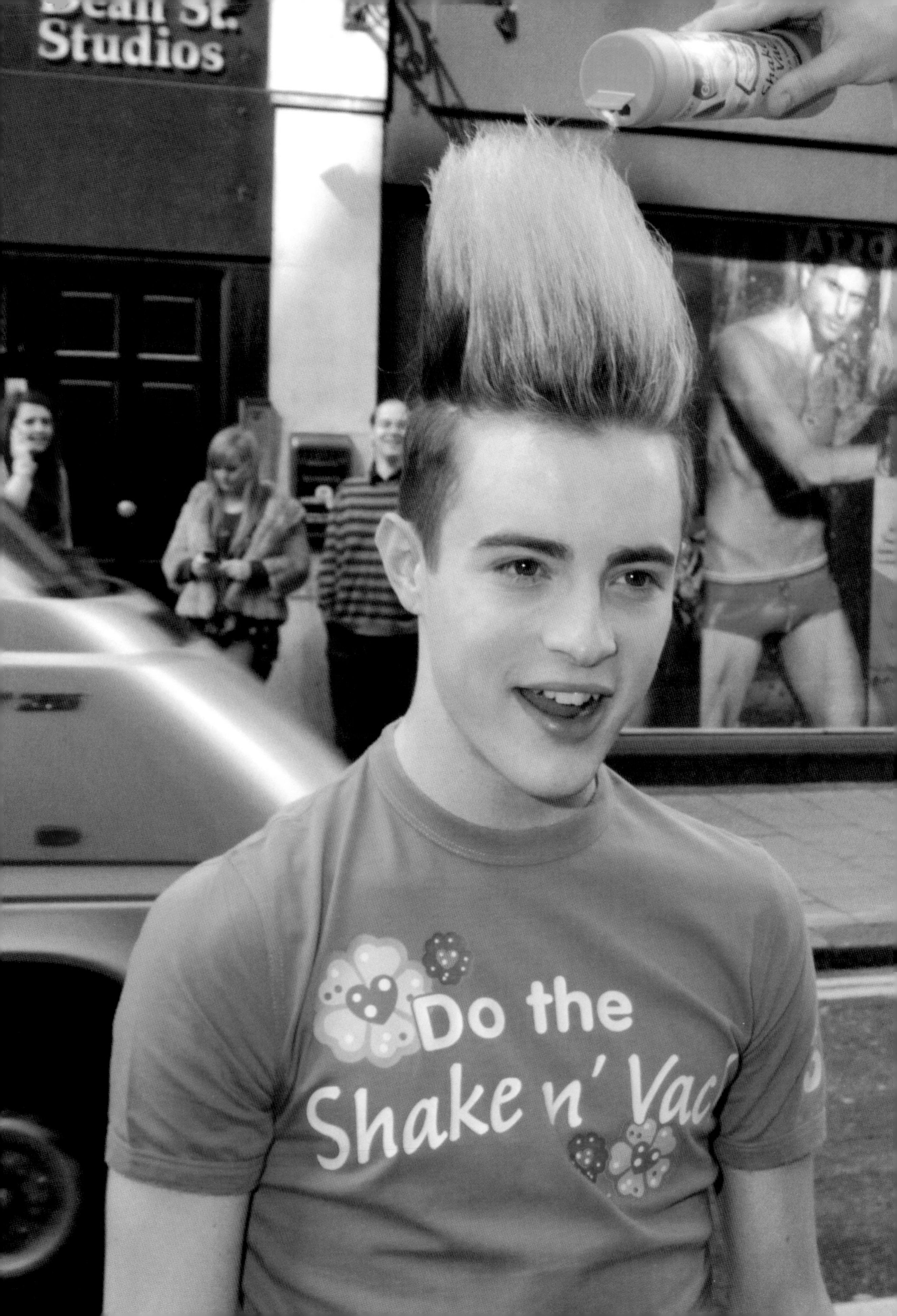
Dean St.
Studios
Do the
Shake n' Vac

CHAPTER FOUR

Lipstick

With their fame in the UK and Ireland sky-high, the twins now wanted to get themselves known further afield. In 2011, John and Edward got a golden opportunity for this when they were chosen to represent their country in the Eurovision Song Contest. They were to compete in the 56th instalment of a contest which has, over the years, launched the careers of musical royalty such as Abba and Celine Dion. Jedward would love to enjoy the sort of global popularity and influence of those winners.

It had been a close finish in the race to represent Ireland. On 12th February, five acts competed for the right to be Ireland's act. It had decided it wanted an already established act, rather than an unknown, to be its entry. The voting was shared by a selected jury and television viewers. John and Edward won by just two votes, their 98 votes allowing them to pip runner-up Nikki Kavanagh who polled 96. So it was that Jedward entered the semi-finals. They were just one step away from the final of the Eurovision Song Contest!

John and Edward were their usual energetic selves at the semi-final in Dusseldorf. On the night the hall seemed to be full of 'Jedwards', thanks to the 3,000 cardboard quiffs that had been delivered

from Ireland that morning, and handed out to audience members. The real twins looked stunning in their red sparkly jackets with big shoulders and tight black trousers. Tens of millions of people were watching, but the twins were far from bowed by this. Instead, they were full of confidence and announced they wanted to be 'the Pavarotti of Eurovision'.

The twins' song for the 2011 contest was **Lipstick**. 'It's a real fast beat, up tempo track, and the minute it starts it goes straight into it, and it's really catchy, and by the end of it you know the chorus,' said John. Could it give them a chance of a win? It is part of Eurovision tradition to include a few 'novelty' acts in the line-up, so there was certainly room for optimism that Jedward and their catchy song would appeal to viewers across Europe.

The boys were excited to be there, though they were never inclined to hide their ambition. 'It's one of the huge competitions in the world,' John also told the **wiwibloggs** website. 'I mean think about it. Every single European country is watching it. And it's a huge way for Jedward to go global.' Edward added: 'Basically we're doing Eurovision because we don't like going on holidays where people don't recognize us. So now we wanna conquer the whole world so people can recognize us in every single country.'

They were not the only identical twins in the competition. Daniela and Veronika Nizlova represented Slovakia under the name TWiiNS - however, they had fallen at the semi-final hurdle. At the press conference ahead of the final, the twins were as full of energy and enthusiasm as ever. They literally leapt onto the desks in the press room. The assembled reporters fell into stitches of laughter as they raved about how excited they were. 'We're one step from meeting Britney Spears,' said John, adding that if they won the Jedward hairstyle could become the 'biggest hairstyle in Europe'. Added Edward: 'We're already a success in UK and Ireland, we can't wait to be a big success all around the world.' They even compared themselves to ABBA and said they wanted to become even bigger than the legendary Swedish pop band.

In the days before the final, Jedward's odds kept getting lower as more and more people began to believe it was Ireland's year. People started to talk about them as favourites, alongside France's tenor Amaury Vassili. There was further good news for them when they learned that a car company in Asia was using *Lipstick* in its television advertisements. They were asked who they would phone first if they won on the night. Edward said they would phone their Mother first, but John said that they would probably actually call Britney Spears. They then proceeded to name a long list of other people they would call including their pet dog, the Pope and Madonna. They eventually said as one: 'Who we gonna call? Ghostbusters!'

They delivered another cracking performance at the final. Around 150 million people were watching and the lads were determined to do themselves proud. They danced and jumped around like two young puppies on a morning walk after a visit to Starbucks. It was a dramatic and memorable performance with a dynamic production. It could have been even more dynamic: they had hoped to have animals, including tigers, on stage with them but they were not allowed to. So they just made up for that with plenty of fun. As *Lipstick* came to a close, the audience in the hall rose as one to hail Ireland's famous twins. This was the most positive audience reaction of the night. Could this be matched in the voting? The boys could only watch and hope.

It was a tense evening as they followed the voting patterns. At times, they remembered the votes they faced in *The X Factor* final. However, this time the voting was taking place across all of Europe. In the early stages of the voting, John and Edward were disappointed to receive low scores. However, they are both optimists and they kept hoping the tide would turn in their favour. So imagine their excitement when they were awarded the maximum 12 points from the UK vote. They soared up the table, overtaking the British act - legendary boy-band Blue. There followed more strong voting for the twins including 12 from Denmark, and they edged even higher up. Spirits soared ever higher as the Irish judge appeared on the monitors wearing a 'Jedward wig'.

But all this excitement was not enough to propel them to victory, which went to the act from Azerbaijan. John and Edward finished in eighth place. To put this in context, it was three places ahead of Blue, who had previously sold 14 million albums around the world. John and Edward had done themselves and Ireland proud. As far as their Manager Louis Walsh was concerned, for Jedward it was not the winning but the taking part that mattered. 'Remember they didn't win **X Factor**', he told the **Belfast Telegraph**. 'This is just another chapter of something that is becoming a worldwide brand. America is next, I think Jedward will be great role models for the kids over there.'

The twins had loved their Eurovision experience. Their performance in front of 150 million television viewers in the final had brought the Jedward experience to a whole new audience and swelled their ever-growing fan-base. Their various releases began to chart in further European nations. They also enjoyed the behind-the-scenes experiences too, including their first ever interviews with translators for foreign-language-speaking viewers. The translators had smiled, taken a deep breath and done their best to keep up with John and Edward's legendary patter.

Who could fail to smile as they watched these two happy-go-lucky boys living out their dreams?

Hello, Mr President

What a year 2011 was proving for John and Edward. Far from fading in popularity as their X Factor journey became a thing of the past, their place in our hearts grew. They were becoming leading lights in the younger markets of the show-business industry. Their status as celebrities was confirmed in May when they performed for none other than the President of the United States of America, Barack Obama, during his two-day visit to Ireland. It was a rainy day in Dublin but that was never going to be enough to dampen their spirits. Indeed, as soon as they appeared on stage the boys lit up the mood of the audience, some of whom had queued overnight to guarantee attendance at the historic event.

They had been so keyed up prior to their performance. 'We're very excited, it's an honour to perform for the most famous man in the world, after Simon Cowell that is,' they told the BBC before hitting the stage. The twins then performed *Lipstick* for the President and the First Lady Michelle Obama on College Green in Dublin. 'You guys rock,' John told the 60,000-strong crowd at the end of their song. 'You guys are awesome!' Who could have imagined as they were booed by X Factor fans in 2009 that two years later they would be such a successful act, invited to perform for the world's most famous leader?

After their performance they raved about the experience on Twitter. They posted: 'It was so cool that @BarackObama liked our Hair! Our hair has been approved by the Biggest person ever. He wanted to know what Jedward meant! We said I'm John and I'm Edward, together we are Jedward!' They added that they had told Michelle Obama that she was 'really cool' and also discussed the Jonas Brothers and Justin Bieber and Miley Cyrus with the President himself - as you do. They had needed plenty of 'swag' to pull-off meeting President Obama and playing it so cool. Fortunately, John and Edward have rarely lacked 'swag'.

Their next major appointment was in the famed *Big Brother* house. The producers of the reality television series had been courting the twins to appear on *Celebrity Big Brother*. With the show moving from Channel 4 to FIVE, the programme-makers were keen for some attention-grabbing headline guests. Who better than Ireland's favourite twins? A deal was struck and it proved a winning formula - from start to finish of their *Big Brother* experience, John and Edward were never less than hilariously entertaining.

They looked striking on launch night, wearing matching tiger costumes they had bought the day before. They were asked if they thought they might irritate their fellow housemates. With a cheeky grin they replied that they 'had no idea' how that might happen, adding: 'I think they'll love our

energy and enthusiasm.' As it turned out, they managed to provoke both love and irritation among the other housemates. Even though they do not drink alcohol themselves, they saw the potential for using drinks for mischief. 'We hear that there is a bar in the house as well,' they told the millions of FIVE viewers before entering. 'We don't drink but we'll be the bartenders and serve everyone, we can get them drunk and make them do silly things!'

Viewers of all ages absolutely adored the boys and their antics from the start. People who had previously ignored or disliked the Grimes brothers were now admitting they had become Jedward fans. Bookmakers quickly named Jedward as their favourites to win. On the housemates' first morning in house, John and Edward were the first to try out the outdoor swimming pool. John tested the water with his toe and told Edward it was heated. This had been a cheeky fib as the water was actually very cold, but it was enough to encourage Edward to join him. They had only been in the pool for a matter of moments before they began to splash each other and generally frolic about. Their older housemates looked on with concern.

Darren was one of the first to turn on them. 'We're going to have to get tougher on them,' he told Sally and Amy after the twins had failed to live up to their promise to clean the house. 'They've got the attention span of a mosquito bite.' They needed all their powers of attention to get through one of the more challenging and memorable tasks set by *Big Brother*. They were called to the diary room and told to change into brightly-coloured cat suits - John's was pink, Edward's was purple. They were told that they would need to separate for the task and make sure the other housemates got to know each of them as individuals. As an extra twist, they were also told they must remain at least five metres apart at all times. If they get too close, they were warned, they would be given an electric shock from the outfits they were wearing.

They set off separately and began to teach the other housemates about the distinctions and differences between them. For instance, John told Darren that he was 10 minutes older than Edward and that his hair was slightly longer. 'I'm also way cooler than Edward,' he said. After leaving Darren, John then leapt on top of Sally who had been trying to sleep on the sofa. Meanwhile, Edward was telling other housemates about his own personal traits. After a while, John found he could no longer resist the temptation to move close to Edward, to test whether they would get electric shocks.

Despite Edward trying to run away from John, the older brother did get close enough to discover that Big Brother's 'electric shock' threat was real. The other housemates burst out laughing as John and Edward received a series of electrical jolts. 'It's a shock,' moaned John, 'it's shocking meee!' For the twins to pass this task, their housemates would need to correctly identify which twin was which from a series of photographs they were shown by Big Brother. The housemates passed the task. Tara was particularly certain in her choices. 'I promise you, one's skinny, one's not,' she said. Big Brother announced that the housemates would be awarded a 'pop party' that evening. As John and Edward returned from the Diary Room, they were mobbed by the jubilant housemates. As they all jumped up and down with glee, it was as if the enthusiastic Jedward spirit had infected everyone in the house.

Then came the day when John 'married' Amy Childs in a mock ceremony. 'Do you promise to love her, to take her everywhere you go, to gel and spike her hair whenever she wants and to take her back to her original roots, Essex?' John was asked. He agreed and they sealed the 'wedding' with a kiss. It had been a bargain basement ceremony: Amy held a bouquet of tissue paper and the rings were made out of tin foil. The 'marriage' was just a joke, but at least it meant that Jedward and Amy made up after a falling-out a few days earlier when the twins had decided to host their own spur-of-the-moment chat show in the living room of the **Big Brother** house. Although the show would be watched by millions of television viewers, John and Edward also wanted a 'studio audience'. So they encouraged their fellow housemates to come and join them.

In the garden, Amy was happily sunbathing alongside Bobby and Pamela. When the twins called out to the housemates in the garden, Amy replied that she was happy to wait until later to join them, as she was enjoying basking in the sun. John decided to take the encouragement a step further and grabbed Amy by her bikini. She was furious and so was Darren, who was sitting nearby and witnessed John's prank. Sally told them that she didn't think John had meant any harm. Later Amy and John made their peace. 'I do love you,' she told John. 'Gimme a cuddle.'

It had been a day of cheeky behaviour from the twins. They had twice made a mess of the kitchen, including spilling a huge jar of coleslaw over the floor. They said they would 'clean it up later,' but it was Kerry who ended up doing that. It was a different story on the day they lost a task and were forced to do the washing-up as the forfeit. Celebrity chef Marco Pierre White had entered the house and he quickly set the housemates the task of cooking one of his favourite dishes - sea bass with chinoise sauce. He gave the housemates a quick cookery lesson and then set them to work on the task. Tara and Lucien were crowned Big Brother's Best Chefs when they won the cooking

challenge. Their reward was a posh private dinner for two. Jedward, though, came last. Even though Pierre White was impressed with their enthusiasm, he said their sea bass with chinoise sauce was the least appetising of the task.

On the night of the final, Jedward finished in third place, behind Kerry Katona who was herself pipped for the top place by *Big Fat Gypsy Wedding* star Paddy Doherty. When the twins left the house they were greeted by cheers from the crowd outside. John told Heatworld that he and his brother believed that their Big Brother experience had been very worthwhile. 'I feel the UK public have more of an understanding of me and Edward and they know what we are about – having loads of fun!' he said. Edward agreed, and said that they were 'totally cool with not winning'. After all, he added, 'Me and John are born winners we can't lose, ok?'

By this stage, their second album was in the shops and being snapped up eagerly by fans, new and old alike. Fittingly for two lads who consider themselves to be eternal winners, it was called Victory...

Victory

The boys had spent the early months of 2011 recording the songs for what would become their second album. The fans could hardly wait for the next release from their beloved brothers. In March they shared a teasing 30-second video of one track, *Bad Behaviour*, with their fans. In June they revealed that the album was complete and that it would consist entirely of original songs. Then, the following month as excitement built, the terrific twins announced it would be called *Victory*.

In July, they released **Bad Behaviour,** which was the second single from the album (after **Lipstick** had been released to coincide with their Eurovision quest). The promotional video featured John and Edward partying wildly in their home after seeing their 'parents' off on holiday. Before they know it, scores of revellers have turned up to the party. The police arrive but the party is so loud that nobody can hear them knocking on the door. The video ends with their parents arriving back full of horror.

The singles **Lipstick** and **Bad Behaviour** are the first two tracks on **Victory**. They very much set the scene for a fun and fantastic album. Over 12 scorching tracks it delights and entertains the listener. The tempo is mostly fast and furious, with **Woh Oh Wow** the only song that takes its foot off the gas slightly. The artwork for the album was, suitably enough, victorious in its theme. It featured the twins wearing white blazers, blue ties and red trainers. Each are cloned in the photograph, meaning it appears as if an endless procession of Jedwards are marching towards the camera.

As for the boys in real life - they continue to march onwards. They are starring in a new television show on CBBC called **Jedward's Tour Of Britain**, will continue modelling for Next Models and generally both maintain and build upon their huge popularity in UK, Ireland and elsewhere in Europe. Meanwhile, their dream of cracking the American market continues. Their manager is convinced they can make it there and several American stars, including Hollywood actress Tara Reid who got to know them in the **Big Brother** house, agree that they are made for the US teenage market.

As for the boys themselves, they have no doubt that America will love them. After all, they have already made friends with the President and have never lacked confidence anyway. Wherever the future takes them, John and Edward Grimes will spread fun and laughter, always approaching life with enthusiasm and energy. They will never forget where they came from. Having been born a couple of months early, they have achieved so much for two young men barely into their twenties.

Whatever you do, don't expect them to slow down anytime soon.